First Facts™

The Solar System

Neptune

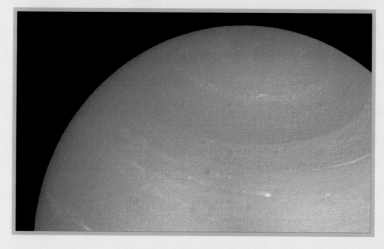

by Ralph Winrich

Consultant:
Stephen J. Kortenkamp, PhD
Research Scientist
Planetary Science Institute, Tucson, Arizona

Capstone
press
Mankato, Minnesota

First Facts is published by Capstone Press,
151 Good Counsel Drive, P.O. Box 669, Mankato, Minnesota 56002.
www.capstonepress.com

Library of Congress Cataloging-in-Publication Data
Winrich, Ralph.
    Neptune / by Ralph Winrich.
    p. cm.—(First facts. The solar system)
    Includes bibliographical references and index.
    ISBN 0-7368-3692-6 (hardcover)
    1. Neptune (Planet)—Juvenile literature. I. Title. II. First facts. Solar system.
QB691.W56 2005
523.481—dc22   2004016436

Summary: Discusses the orbit, atmosphere, surface features, and exploration of Neptune.

Editorial Credits
Gillia Olson, editor; Juliette Peters, designer and illustrator; Jo Miller, photo researcher;
    Scott Thoms, photo editor

Photo Credits
Astronomical Society of the Pacific/NASA, 14, 15
Corbis/Bettmann, 20 (right)
Digital Vision, 16–17
Getty Images/Hulton Archive, 20 (left)
NASA/JPL, 5
Photodisc, cover, 1, 4, planet images within illustrations and chart, 6–7, 10, 13, 19, 21
Photo Researchers Inc./Science Photo Library/NASA, 9
Space Images/NASA/STScl, 16 (inset)

1 2 3 4 5 6 10 09 08 07 06 05

Table of Contents

Voyager 2 and Neptune

Without a **telescope**, Neptune cannot be seen from Earth. With a telescope, Neptune looks like a tiny circle. People finally got a close-up view of the planet in 1989. The *Voyager 2* **spacecraft** flew by it and took pictures. Clouds swirl around this faraway planet.

Fast Facts about Neptune

Diameter: 30,760 miles (49,500 kilometers)
Average Distance from Sun: 2.8 billion miles (4.5 billion kilometers)
Average Temperature (cloud top): minus 279 degrees Fahrenheit (minus 173 degrees Celsius)
Length of Day: 16 hours, 7 minutes
Length of Year: 164 Earth years, 10 months
Moons: 13
Rings: 5 or 6

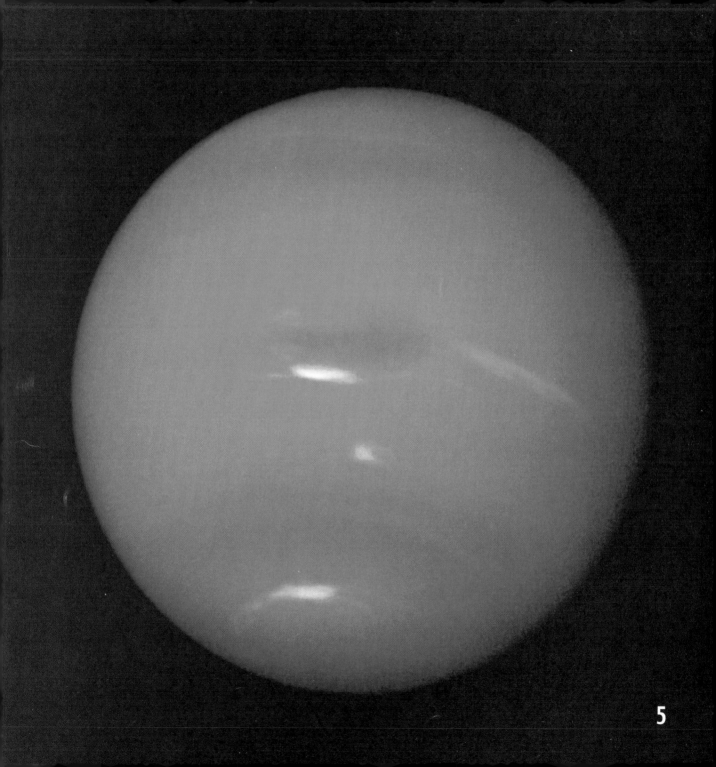

5

The Solar System

Neptune is the eighth planet from the Sun. It is the smallest of the four giant planets. Jupiter, Saturn, and Uranus are the other giant planets.

The rest of the planets are smaller than Neptune. Mercury, Venus, Earth, and Mars are the closest planets to the Sun. Pluto, the smallest of all, lies past Neptune.

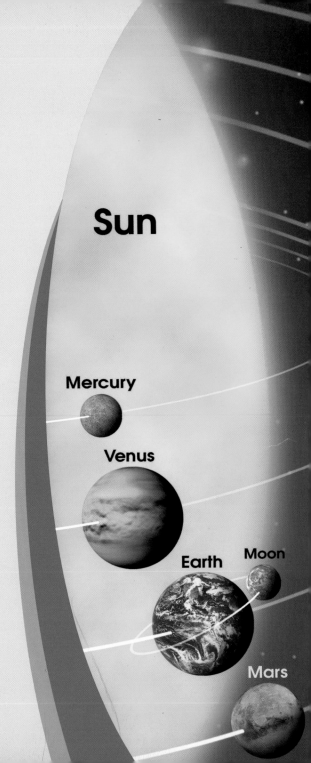

Sun

Mercury

Venus

Earth

Moon

Mars

Jupiter

Saturn

Uranus

Pluto

Neptune

Neptune's Atmosphere

A planet's **atmosphere** is made up of the gases that surround it. Neptune's atmosphere is mostly hydrogen, helium, and methane. Methane gas makes the planet look blue.

Wispy, white clouds move quickly around Neptune's atmosphere. They cast shadows on the thick clouds below.

! Fun Fact!
Wind speeds on Neptune are faster than on any other planet.

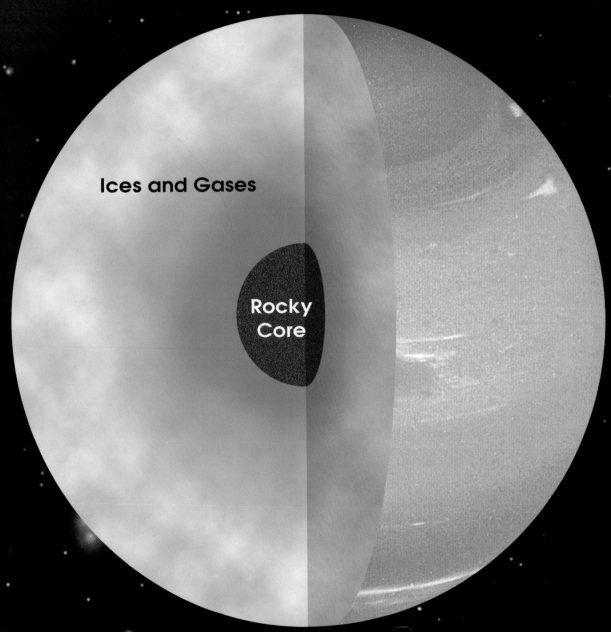

Ices and Gases

Rocky
Core

Neptune's Makeup

Neptune is mostly made up of ice and gas. Neptune's only solid part is its rocky **core**. The rest of the planet is a thick soupy mixture of ice and gas.

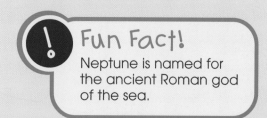

Fun Fact!
Neptune is named for the ancient Roman god of the sea.

How Neptune Moves

As Neptune circles the Sun, it spins on its **axis**. Neptune takes nearly 165 Earth years to circle the Sun. Neptune spins once in 16 hours, 7 minutes.

Neptune is sometimes the ninth planet from the Sun. Neptune's path around the Sun sometimes takes it farther away than Pluto.

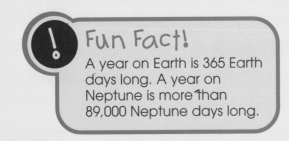

Fun Fact!
A year on Earth is 365 Earth days long. A year on Neptune is more than 89,000 Neptune days long.

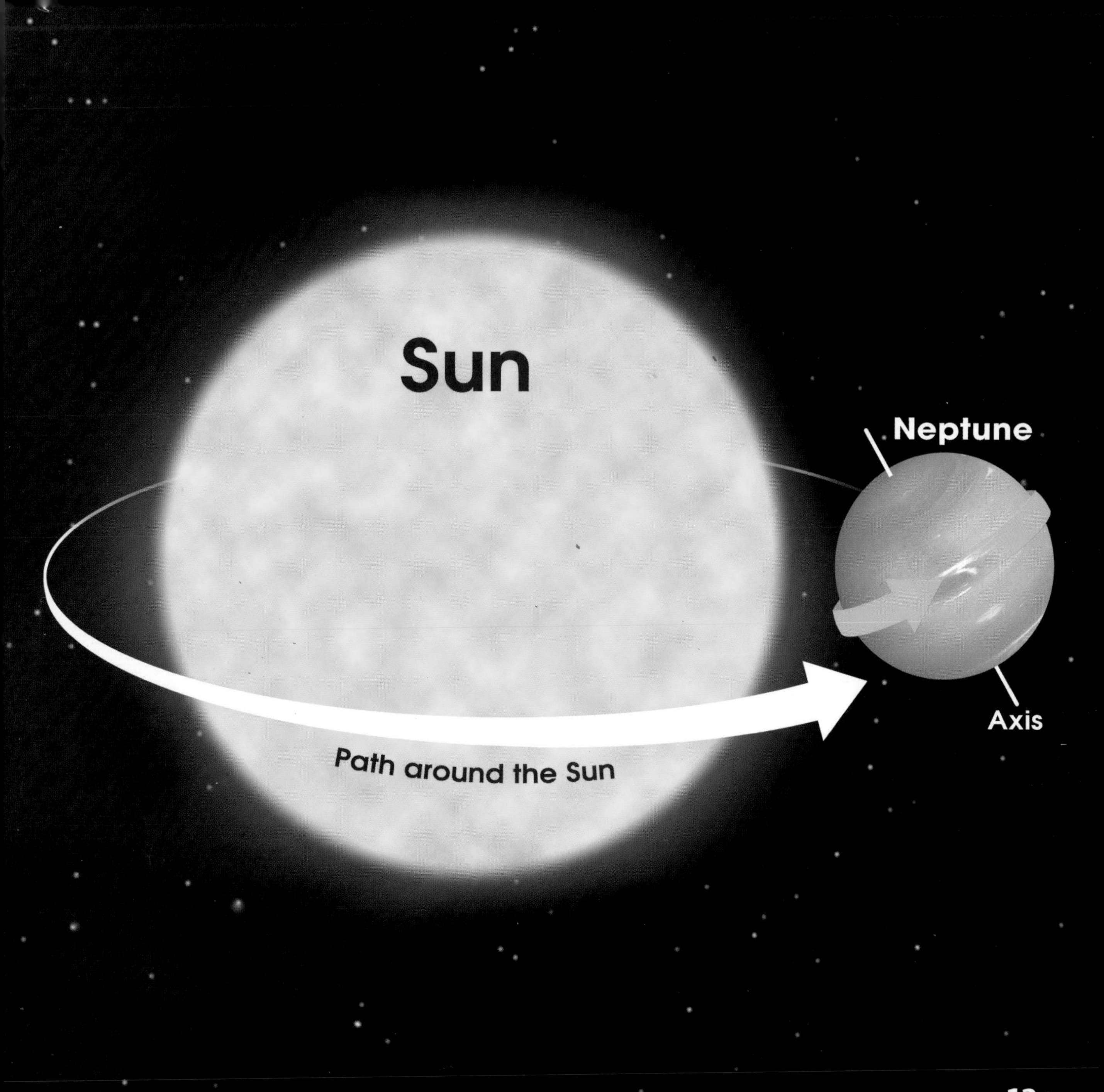

Sun

Neptune

Path around the Sun

Axis

geyser on
Triton

Moons and Rings

Neptune has 13 moons. The largest
moon is Triton. Triton has a thin
atmosphere. It also has **geysers** that
shoot out black clouds of gas and dust.

Neptune has faint rings made of dust. One ring seems to be only half there. Scientists aren't sure if Neptune has five rings or six rings.

Pictures from Hubble

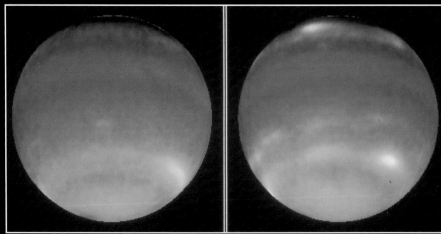

Studying Neptune

Scientists have no plans to send more spacecraft to Neptune. Today, scientists use telescopes to study the planet. The Hubble Space Telescope has shown new cloud features on Neptune.

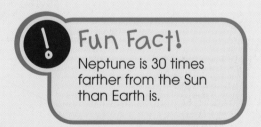

Fun Fact!
Neptune is 30 times farther from the Sun than Earth is.

Comparing Neptune to Earth

Neptune and Earth are very different. Earth is a rocky planet. Neptune is a soupy mixture of gas and ice. Neptune's atmosphere is filled with gases that are **poisonous** to people. People can't live there. Instead, scientists will continue to study this strange world from afar.

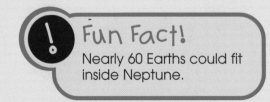

Fun Fact!

Nearly 60 Earths could fit inside Neptune.

Size Comparison

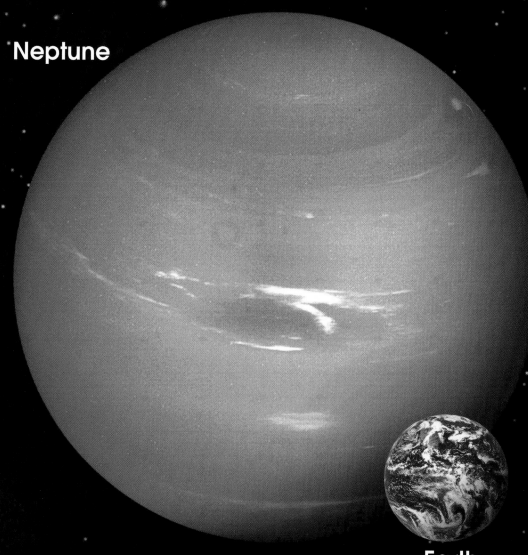

Neptune

Earth

Amazing but True!

The people who discovered Neptune didn't actually see it. In the 1840s, John Couch Adams and Urbain Le Verrier thought an unknown planet was affecting Uranus' movement. They used math to figure out where the new planet would be found. In 1846, other scientists used this information to spot Neptune with telescopes.

Adams

Le Verrier

Planet Comparison Chart

Planet	Size Rank (1=largest)	Makeup	1 Trip around the Sun (Earth Time)
Mercury	8	rock	88 days
Venus	6	rock	225 days
Earth	5	rock	365 days, 6 hours
Mars	7	rock	687 days
Jupiter	1	gases and ice	11 years, 11 months
Saturn	2	gases and ice	29 years, 6 months
Uranus	3	gases and ice	84 years
Neptune	4	gases and ice	164 years, 10 months
Pluto	9	rock and ice	248 years

Glossary

atmosphere (AT-muhss-feehr)—the layer of gases that surrounds some planets and moons

axis (AK-siss)—an imaginary line that runs through the middle of a planet or moon; a planet spins on its axis.

core (KOR)—the inner part of a planet that is made of metal or rock

geyser (GYE-zur)—a hole in the ground where gas and dust shoot up in bursts

poisonous (POI-zuhn-uhss)—harmful if swallowed or breathed in

spacecraft (SPAYSS-kraft)—a vehicle that travels in space

telescope (TEL-uh-skope)—an instrument that makes faraway objects appear larger and closer

Read More

Hayhurst, Chris. *Neptune.* The Library of the Nine Planets. New York: Rosen, 2005.

Rau, Dana Meachen. *Neptune.* Our Solar System. Minneapolis: Compass Point Books, 2003.

Waxman, Laura Hamilton. *Neptune.* Our Universe. Minneapolis: Lerner, 2003.

Internet Sites

FactHound offers a safe, fun way to find Internet sites related to this book. All of the sites on FactHound have been researched by our staff.

Here's how:
1. Visit *www.facthound.com*
2. Type in this special code **0736836926** for age-appropriate sites. Or enter a search word related to this book for a more general search.
3. Click on the **Fetch It** button.

FactHound will fetch the best sites for you!

Index